Cabin Days

DESIRAE J. CRAM

authorHOUSE

AuthorHouse™
1663 Liberty Drive
Bloomington, IN 47403
www.authorhouse.com
Phone: 833-262-8899

Published by AuthorHouse 04/04/2022

ISBN: 978-1-6655-5634-7 (sc)
ISBN: 978-1-6655-5633-0 (e)

Print information available on the last page.

Any people depicted in stock imagery provided by Getty Images are models, and such images are being used for illustrative purposes only. Certain stock imagery © Getty Images.

This book is printed on acid-free paper.

Because of the dynamic nature of the Internet, any web addresses or links contained in this book may have changed since publication and may no longer be valid. The views expressed in this work are solely those of the author and do not necessarily reflect the views of the publisher, and the publisher hereby disclaims any responsibility for them.

Contents

Dedication

This book is dedicated to any and all who've adventured with me. May you never lose your wonder.

Stillness

My little Earth stands still
While I look out at the trees
Across the hill
The fire in the hearth dances
As if rehearsed

Black coffee I sip at ease
Mornings like these portray my will
Or is it God's will

To stand still
With the trees
Sipping with ease

While the warmth fills my heart
Maybe some morning I will come to know
God's great and powerful will

Is life to stand at ease
Maybe it is
Maybe it's not
Oh, how my heart dances
For mornings like these

WONDER TIME

What makes your heart dance in the morning?

True Dance

Today I cried
As a matter of fact, I wept
It made sense
Crying and weeping
The Earth was in on it too
In fact, we had a party
Streamers of tears fell down
As the celebration rang through the trees
We all agreed
It was time to weep
After the sky cried
And I cried
We all got dry

Then I looked up
Being reminded
There is a time to weep
A time to dance

The sky was not taking a chance

After a good cry
For the dance

WONDER TIME

What brings you out of a place of sadness?

Moon and Loon

Hello moon
Stretching out on the lake
Hello loon
Searching for your mate
Some things you just can't take
So, I sit in awe
Of the moon and the loon
Simply being
On the lake

WONDER TIME

What animal brings you awe and why?

Laughter

Oh, to laugh
To deeply laugh
Where you feel the inside of you curl
This is true laughter

Breathing so hard you can't keep up
All of a sudden there's silence
Or you bark like a seal

In a moment, everything is paused
You turn inside out

WONDER TIME

How would you describe the sound and feeling of your laugh?

Water

Shining, like a show of glorious northern lights
Dancing while on display
Constantly moving
Ever-changing
Roaring
Fierce
Like a lioness
Still
Paused
Like a sleeping babe
Speckled
Smooth
Chopped
Maybe with a ripple

These are the many faces of water
Go and see

I hear there's more

WONDER TIME

What adjective would you use to describe the face of water and why?

Young Woman

As she sways
Back and forth
Back and forth

The wind catches her hair
Sweet tunes draw near

Oh, how great is her worth
He knows of course
Of how great is her worth

He will not let her fall
Into the follower's snare

Because he calls her dear
Be at rest young woman
As you sway

Back and forth
Back and forth

WONDER TIME

How does it make you feel knowing you have inherit worth?

Cliff Jumping

Sometimes you step
Sometimes you fall
Sometimes you leap
To then, not move at all
After a while
You answer the call
With gumption and all
You fall
Through the air
Into the water

 DESIRAE J. CRAM

WONDER TIME

Have you ever been cliff jumping? Describe
that experience and how it felt.

The Smokehaus

There was sunshine and rocks
Waves, wind, and people

The rush of people
The lines filled with people
"What sandwich should we get?"
The smoked maple-sage turkey
"To go please."
While I sat where

There was sunshine and rocks
Waves, wind, and people

Do not waste a moment of creativity
You'll experience regret
Sometimes creativity is
Smoked maple-sage turkey
With cranberry walnut sauce on rye
Sometimes it's where

There is sunshine and rocks
Waves, wind and people

WONDER TIME

What does creativity look like for you?

Bravery

To believe
Truly believe
And to know of
God's love
And goodness in your life
Is the epitome

Of bravery

 DESIRAE J. CRAM

WONDER TIME

What comes to mind when you think of the idea of bravery?

Winter Woods

Icicles hung three feet long
Pine needles dance in the wind
Branches drop clumps of snow

You wake up
But the outside is fast asleep
Covered in blankets, dustings, and mounds
Of wet and frosty white

Night is gone
And the sun offers it's light
Inside everything is right

Coffee in hand
And the fire
Crackling in sight

Night is gone
The winter woods
Are just right
In sight

  DESIRAE J. CRAM

WONDER TIME

What comes alive for you during the winter months?

Or Was That Joy

Today was full of glee
We shouted "yippee"
For our favorite broomball team
Down the hill
We went for a ski
The sun was out
Passing along greetings
Through its beams
The steam from the sauna
Warmed us from the inside out
Or was that joy
As we jumped to and fro
From the lake to the shore

Joy
All the more

WONDER TIME

What does it look like for you to experience true joy?

Your Face

It's been someday
Trying to move along
I see your face
Lying out here in the sun

I'm so tired of moving on
Maybe someday
I'll belong

WONDER TIME

Describe the contrast of belonging and not belonging.
How have you seen this play out in your life?

Spring

It is here
It is near, some say
It has sprung

The skies are clear
Soon the lakes will be
Like a mirror
The icicles are no longer hung

Round and round go the birds
Circling the newly filled feeders

The deer are out and about
As if they're the town greeters

This is what you do
I have arrived
You make me come alive

Even the birds and the deer
Know you are here
You are near

Spring is here

Or maybe something more

WONDER TIME

What type of anticipation does Spring bring in your life?

Cedar

There are rocks and leaves
And Cedar trees
Holding their own
In the breeze

Lying low
They cover the seas

Oh wait
That's a lake
Basswood, you might say
Goes on for days

Paddling to and fro
From bay to bay

Travel surely fills up your day
After the wind and waves
Have had their say
I find myself eager

To rest under
The great Cedar trees

WONDER TIME

After a hard day of travel or work what brings the most rest to your soul?

What a Morning

Have you ever sat in wonder?
Contemplating a mystery
While feeling the warm sun on your face
As it rises over the trees
Then there's the sounds

Birds
Crickets
Loons

Every little thing that goes on nameless
It's almost as if the lake is dancing
Yet simultaneously so still
Have the clouds dropped down from the sky?
I see now that's just fog

But not just fog
Really
There's abundantly more

WONDER TIME

What mystery of creation puts you in a state of wonder?

Runaway

So, then I leave
Only to be found
In the still and quiet woods
Under the trees and against a rock
Where one can think

And I do think

There's much to pray about

WONDER TIME

What type of environment brings forth the best thinking?

Temporary Community

Built together
From the red pines in the forest
Root in root
Standing tall
We're not perfect
But with each other
We're better
To bring glory
To the king
Above all

WONDER TIME

What aspects of community have you experienced?
Have they been positive or negative? Do you participate
in an active community? Why, or why not?

Winter Solstice

My God
Your truths and promises
Speak
Throughout all
Creation

WONDER TIME

What about creation speaks to you?

That Will Do

A few words have been spoken
That is just enough
Many more would be too much
Today
Unlike many and most
Is made for thinking
Completely through
Tomorrow
Sounds will come
Sure enough in me
And you too
For now, there's silence

And that dear friend will do

WONDER TIME

Take a moment to sit in silence. Acknowledge how you feel and what you think of in this space.

Rhythm

Have you noticed or seen?
The sun rises and falls

No one ever questions

Yet God, the only one
Promised to love us
Through and through

We question
You and I

Whether he loves us at all?
Why do bad things happen?
Why does the sun fall?

God have mercy on us all

WONDER TIME

Take some time to think about what in life is constant, and yet maybe you take for granted?

Grace

How easily I forget
God's grace on humanity
His deep, deep love
For his children
I need a reminder
To be thrashed at me
A river, with its ever flowing
Deep, deep waters
Is just what I need
To see a glimpse
Of grace

WONDER TIME

What reminds you of God's love?

Creation

Creation has a marvelous story to tell
Not only thousands of years ago
But today
Right now
Listen

WONDER TIME

Take some time to sit and listen intently to the world around you. Write down what you hear.

The Waltz

So, then we go
Only to wait
To move forward
Just to pause
There is excitement
And a stall
Eagerness to push through
And wondering that brings a halt
These are rhythms
Immune to none
And friends to all

WONDER TIME

What are rhythms in your life that you appreciate? If you have none what are some that you could incorporate into your daily routines?

February Buds

The snow is falling
Somewhere the buds are calling
To be let go
Of winter's stronghold
They wait in anticipation
Of what is new
Wanting to come
But not wanting to break through
February is here
Somehow the trees begin to look new
Then pause
And wait
Now look
The little red buds are here
It is true

WONDER TIME

What are some things you need to let go of in order for new to come?

Kindness

The lake is still, quiet, and calm
It invites the soul to come
When it's roaring, crashing, and loud
We see strength come from the calm
The strength isn't inviting
We need the calm
There's kindness here
To be found

WONDER TIME

What does it look like for you to embrace the calm?

www.ingramcontent.com/pod-product-compliance
Lightning Source LLC
Chambersburg PA
CBHW051417250726
48655CB00003B/1099